LET'S·READ·AND·FIND·OUT·SCIENCE®

SLEEP
is for everyone

by Paul Showers · illustrated by Wendy Watson

HarperCollinsPublishers

STAGE 1

The *Let's-Read-and-Find-Out Science* book series was originated by Dr. Franklyn M. Branley, Astronomer Emeritus and former Chairman of the American Museum–Hayden Planetarium, and was formerly co-edited by him and Dr. Roma Gans, Professor Emeritus of Childhood Education, Teachers College, Columbia University. Text and illustrations for each of the books in the series are checked for accuracy by an expert in the relevant field. For more information about Let's-Read-and-Find-Out Science books, write to HarperCollins Children's Books, 10 East 53rd Street, New York, NY 10022.

Sleep Is for Everyone

Library of Congress Cataloging-in-Publication Data
Showers, Paul.
  Sleep is for everyone / by Paul Showers ; illustrated by Wendy Watson. — (Newly illustrated ed.)
     p.   cm. — (Let's-read-and-find-out science. Stage 1)
  Summary: Discusses the importance of sleep and what happens to our brains and bodies during slumber.
  ISBN 0-06-025392-4. — ISBN 0-06-025393-2 (lib. bdg.). — ISBN 0-06-445141-0 (pbk.)
  1. Sleep—Juvenile literature. (1. Sleep.) I. Watson, Wendy, ill. II. Title. III. Series.
QP425.S58   1997
612.8'21—dc21   96-49375
                                                                                                       CIP
                                                                                                       AC

Typography by Alicia Mikles
1 2 3 4 5 6 7 8 9 10
❖
First Edition

SLEEP
is for everyone

When a horse goes to sleep, its eyelids go down.

When a chicken goes to sleep, its eyelids go up. When a snake sleeps, its eyes stay open. Snakes have no eyelids.

When you go to sleep, which way do your eyelids go?

5

An elephant can sleep standing up.

A pigeon sits down when it sleeps. Pigs lie down to sleep. So do dogs. So do you. Sometimes dogs curl up. So do cats. Cows don't.

Do you?

Like birds and animals, people have to sleep. Some people sleep more than others. Jonathan is only six weeks old. He sleeps most of the time. He only wakes up when he wants to eat—or have his diaper changed.

Caroline is two years old. She goes to bed right after her dinner. She sleeps all night, twelve hours or more. She takes a nap in the afternoon, too.

When Caroline doesn't get her nap, she is cranky. She cries. She throws things. But the next morning she feels fine—after she's had a good night's sleep.

When people are little, they are growing, and they need a lot of sleep. As they grow bigger and older, they need less sleep. Schoolchildren need to sleep about ten to twelve hours a night.

Most grown-ups need only seven or eight hours. But babies, children, and grown-ups—all of them need to have their sleep.

Every part of your body has to rest after it does its work. Your arms need to rest after they carry heavy bundles. When you run fast, your legs work hard. They get tired, and you have to rest them.

Your brain works hard, too. It never stops working. When you are awake, it helps you pay attention to the world around you—to the sights you see and the sounds you hear, and to the things you taste and smell and feel. You can sit perfectly still and rest your arms and legs, but your brain isn't resting. It goes right on thinking as long as you are awake.

At night your brain needs a rest from thinking. It needs to turn off the world—the way you turn off the light when you go to bed. Sleep is the time when part of your brain takes a rest.

Some parts of your brain keep working even when you are asleep. Your brain keeps your heart beating and your lungs breathing. But your eyes are shut, and they don't see. Your ears are open, but you don't hear many sounds. Your brain doesn't think wide-awake thoughts when you sleep. But it dreams.

Scientists have tried to find out what would happen if people didn't get enough sleep. The scientists didn't go to bed. They stayed up all night and all the next day, and all that night and the day after that.

They grew very sleepy. It was harder and harder to stay awake. They tried to read—but they couldn't follow the words. They tried to look at TV—but their eyes kept closing. They played games—but they made mistakes.

It was harder and harder for their tired brains to think. The scientists grew cross and mean. They got mad at their friends. They kept walking around the room so they wouldn't fall asleep. They drank coffee. They kept yawning.

Finally the scientists were too tired to stand up any longer. When they sat down, they fell asleep in their chairs. They simply couldn't stay awake anymore.

If people stay awake too long, they don't feel well. Scientists do not know exactly why sleep is good for people, but they know that all people need it to be healthy and to feel good.

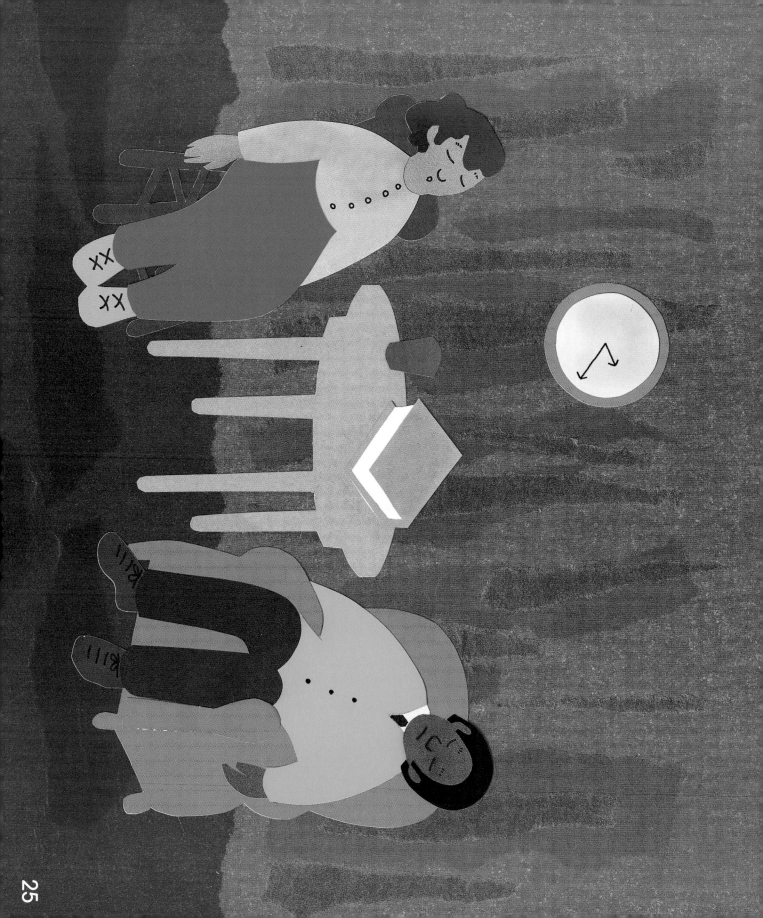

Sometimes it is hard to go to bed. Perhaps I want to watch something on TV. But my mother makes me go to bed. Sometimes she is cross with me. That's because she is tired. Sometimes I'm cross. That's because I'm tired.

Most of the time
I go to bed when my
parents tell me. It is
warm under the covers.
Sometimes I curl up.
Or I stretch out and twist
around. I yawn. I shut my
eyes. I feel as if I am floating.

My thoughts begin to wander. I am floating on a rubber mattress in a pool . . . or in a balloon high up in the clouds. I think of different things—riding my bicycle . . . roller-skating . . . an airplane high in the sky . . . a basket of apples . . . waves at the seashore . . . racing cars . . . my goldfish. . . .

Soon I stop thinking. I am asleep.